Bonsai

JOCHEN PFISTERER

Series Editor:
LESLEY YOUNG

MEREHURST

Contents

An enchanting picture – a group of trees in miniature.

Correct wiring needs practice.

Shaping.

Repot a bonsai every one to two years.

Introduction

In recent years interest in bonsai has been on the increase as more and more plant lovers have discovered just how decorative these miniature trees are when grown indoors. Such plants must be chosen with care, however, because although indoor bonsai are normal woody plants just like outdoor bonsai, which have been shaped according to certain rules, it is really only species that originate from warm climates (such as the tropics, subtropics and Mediterranean regions) that feel comfortable when grown inside our homes. Caring for these tiny trees is not too difficult if you buy the right species of plant to begin with and learn how to care for them and how to keep your bonsai growing in the right shape.

This colourful guide will introduce you to 50 of the most suitable plants for growing as indoor bonsai. All of these plants are illustrated with splendid photographs that were specially taken for this volume. Clear instructions on care explain how to encourage your bonsai to grow well and take on the desired shape.

In addition to choosing the right kind of plant, it is also important for these little trees to be watered, fertilized and repotted in the right way, while, of course, their shape must also be maintained and improved. In this guide, Jochen Pfisterer, a biologist and experienced bonsai gardener, tells you all you need to know about caring for bonsai and explains how to shape them in simple, easy-to-follow terms. By using photographs of correctly shaped indoor bonsai, the author demonstrates all the most important bonsai styles. When it comes to main-

taining the shape of a bonsai and also improving it, through pruning and wiring, all the necessary procedures are illustrated in step-by-step photographs, so that what may at first glance seem extremely complicated will soon yield problem-free results. Further instructions and helpful photographs are used to explain all the other things you need to know about bonsai care so that even a beginner will not find it too difficult to care for an indoor bonsai and, depending on the species, may even coax it into flower. Furthermore, as even indoor bonsai may occasionally become infested with pests, the author has included precise instructions for toxin-free pest control.

Good advice about caring for and shaping existing bonsai is not all that this book offers. It will also take the reader one step further, by giving an excellent introduction to the "high art" of bonsai growing. First, however, the author shows how you can shape a bonsai yourself using an ordinary pot plant. In this way, you can learn the techniques of the artistic side of the hobby of bonsai growing and should eventually pluck up enough courage to have a go at more complicated experiments in shaping real bonsai.

The author
Jochen Pfisterer is a biologist and gardener, co-owner of a bonsai nursery and a contributor to the German gardening magazine *Mein Schöner Garten*. He has spent over ten years in growing and shaping bonsai plants and gives regular lectures and instructional courses on bonsai growing.

Acknowledgements
The author and publishers wish to thank everyone who has contributed towards the creation of this book, especially Jürgen Stork, Andreas Riedmiller and all the other many plant photographers for their exceptionally beautiful and informative photographs.
Special thanks go to Paul Lesniewicz of the Bonsai Centre in Heidelberg, who supplied the majority of the indoor bonsai plants depicted here.

Attractive orange jasmine
This Murraya paniculata, shaped in the twin-trunk style (SOKAN), is about 40 years old and over 50 cm (20 in) tall. It flowers in early summer and has white, sweetly scented, starlike flowers.

Bonsai – an enchanted world in miniature

Bonsai are miniature trees which have been shaped out of ordinary woody plants or trees. Plants from the warmer regions of the world are used to create indoor bonsai – from the tropics, subtropics and regions with a Mediterranean climate. Many of these trees are also used as large container plants for patios. In the Far East the art of bonsai has been practised for over a thousand years.

What is a bonsai?

The word bonsai is made up of two Japanese pictographs, "bon" meaning dish or bowl and "sai" meaning tree. Translated literally, this becomes "pot tree" or "large container tree". In reality, however, bonsai are meant to represent idealized images of full-grown, ancient trees and have often attained their particular shape through years of steady work, sometimes spanning several human generations. The plants that are used are young trees, about 4-6 m (13-20 ft) tall, which have branched out well just above the root system. Through skilled pruning and gentle shaping with the help of wire, they gradually attain their desired shape.

The origins of bonsai

Bonsai were first created in China over a thousand years ago. The two pictographs that make up the Chinese name are the same as the Japanese ones, but the Chinese read them as "pen-jing" rather than as "bon-sai".

The philosophy behind the art of bonsai is the Buddhist belief that all things on Earth – rocks, plants, animals and people – are reborn over and over again. This means that a stone may become a person, a person may become a plant in their next life, and so on. In this way, by striving for the highest possible state of spiritual perfection in one's previous incarnation, it should be possible to attain the next highest rung on the ladder of being in one's next incarnation. The principal way of achieving a state of inner peace and detachment is through regular meditation and one of the methods of meditating is to spend hours quietly gazing at a tree growing in the wild. It is thus quite possible that bonsai trees were first developed for reasons of convenience, while the creation of miniature trees in bowls also offered the opportunity to collect different types and shapes of trees.

The first bonsai

There is a charming story which connects the creation of the art of bonsai with the ancient fashion among Chinese ladies at the imperial court of binding their feet. Gautama Buddha had a habit of meditating and preaching in the shade of certain large trees. These trees later became places of pilgrimage after the Buddha's death. When the religion he had founded spread to the Far East, many existing tree sanctuaries were reconsecrated as places of Buddhist veneration.

In about AD 60 the entire Chinese imperial court converted to Buddhism and a change then took place with respect to the tree sanctuaries. In order to avoid mixing with the great crowds of pilgrims at these sanctuaries, Chinese aristocrats began to create replicas of these holy trees and, indeed, entire landscapes, in their own private gardens. In order to do this, gardeners had to plant relatively young trees and then shape them over time into miniature copies of their sacred models.

From the eleventh century onwards, the ladies of the imperial court took to binding their feet to keep them tiny. As they then could not walk, they had to be carried into the gardens to meditate. A particularly imaginative gardener is supposed to have hit upon the bright idea of taking the trees to the ladies instead. He would choose a particularly small tree and plant it in a large container for easy transport. Thus the "penjing/bonsai" was born.

Bonsai for all weathers

This new development provided excellent opportunities for meditation. As one could now amass large collections of these little trees, it became possible to keep a tree in readiness for any kind of weather – rugged pines looking as if they were being lashed by a storm or bearing dead branches as though in the grip of harsh winter weather, dainty maple trees and flowering cherry trees for mild spring days, and so on.

An interesting semi-cascade (HAN-KENGAI): "The tree of a thousand stars" – Serissa foetida from southern China.

The beginnings of Japanese bonsai

Around AD 1200, Chinese ambassadors took the first "penjing" plants to Japan. The Japanese courtiers became ecstatic about these potted trees, which they called bonsai, and soon overtook their teachers in the further development of this new artform. During the course of the next 800 years, they developed the multitude of new shapes and techniques with which we are now familiar.

A bonsai should look as old and gnarled as possible, as if it has been standing up to wind and weather for centuries. The crown is shaped to look fairly open, so that the branches and stem are clearly visible. The top of the root system should also be exposed, like that of a tree growing in the forest. The dainty bowl or dish is chosen to provide a harmonious, complementary finish to the total picture.

Original plants

In their countries of origin, bonsai are nearly always wild plants or trees. This is because of their original importance as aids to meditation. The small tree was supposed to help the observer to relax and put him or her into a mood that corresponded with existing weather patterns. Indoors, a particular tree would be placed in a special position for only a few hours or days at a time. Usually, the collection itself was kept outside, mainly for reasons of space. Nowadays, bonsai is a very secular hobby, even in Japan, as few people take the time to meditate.

Indoor bonsai

Europeans have a different relationship to plants. They are used to cultivating indoor pot plants all year round, leaving trees to grow outside in the garden. For this reason, western gardeners prefer to use plants for bonsai which can be kept indoors all year round, do not mind central heating and might only go outside in the summer. The basic plant used for indoor bonsai is, therefore, generally a woody plant from tropical and subtropical regions, for example, from southern Japan and southern China, the tropical rain forests, the dry plains of Australia or from the Mediterranean countries. Most of these plants are species that we have long been familiar with as house plants or large container plants.

Rules for shaping a bonsai

There are certain rules which govern the shaping of bonsai. The ratio of the dimensions of the crown to the trunk of the tree are determined just as surely as the ideal position of the tree in its bowl. The same goes for the number of plants in a group planting.

The Lo-Shu Square

A square that has been divided into nine equal parts (see illustration) is used to symbolize heaven (centre) and the eight cardinal points of the compass. These numbers (from 1 to 9) are meant to represent particular characteristics of these eight directions. The sum of each row of figures yields the number 15.

The ideal position in a bowl: The 5 in the centre of the Lo-Shu Square is seen as the seat of the gods. The points closest to the gods are the junctions of the outer squares with the inner square. This makes these the ideal points for the position of the plant in its bowl.

Ratios of dimensions: The ideal proportions of a bonsai are also predetermined through the use of the Lo-Shu Square. The central row of numbers (7, 5, 3) is used in this calculation. This means that the ratio of the total height of the tree, to the crown, to the height of the stem should be 7:5:3. Example: A tree that is 21 cm (just over 8 in) in height should ideally have a crown that is 15 cm (6 in) in diameter and a stem that is 9 cm (3 in) high. Even the size of the bowl can be calculated on this principle – the ratio of the diameter of the crown or the height of the tree to the length of the bowl should be 7:5. A tree 28 cm (11 in) high should therefore be planted in a bowl that is 20 cm (8 in) long.

Groups of plants: If you use the numbers 7,5,3, a group of eight trees should be divided into two groups of five and three trees. In a group of three trees, the trees themselves could be of different heights in a ratio of 7:5:3 (for example, 35 cm/14 in, 25 cm/10 in and 15 cm/6 in).

The Lo-Shu Square, a model for the harmony of the cosmos. The sum of each row is 15. The number 5 is the central seat of the gods.

The Fibonacci series

The second important series of numbers is the Fibonacci series, a string of numbers in which each successive number is found by adding the two numbers immediately preceding it: 0, 1, 1, 2, 3, 5, 8, 13, 21, 34 and so on. Following this principle, three trees should, therefore, be planted in two groups of one and two trees. A group of five plants should be divided into one group containing two trees and another group containing three.

Different shapes

As the bonsai was originally conceived as an aid to meditation, it should serve to draw the attention of the observer closer to the energies of nature. For this reason, the various shapes of Japanese bonsai are not artistic in the sense that they are freely created shapes but have always been derived from models in the wild.

Copies of natural trees

A well-shaped bonsai should look like an exact copy of a large tree that you might find in the wild. If you place a bonsai in front of a landscape background and cover up the bowl, you should be able to create the impression that the bonsai is part of that landscape. There are a few clues, however, which always give the game away. A bonsai will never have as many fine twigs as a large tree, nor are its leaves or needles small enough to correspond to its miniaturized dimensions. A bonsai is not, therefore, an exact copy but rather an abstract image of the natural tree.

A bonsai is grown in a flat bowl or a tall, slender container. The flat bowl symbolizes a flat piece of rock or a meadow. The tall containers, which are used for cascades, represent steep rocks from which the trees protrude.

Group style: a Sageretia thea 30 years old and 45 cm (18 in) tall.

Twin-trunk style: a Sageretia thea 45 years old and 35 cm (14 in) tall.

The most important shapes in Japanese bonsai are introduced in the following text and photographs. The English and/or Latin names are given, as well as the Japanese name and the symbolic or philosophical connotation of the style.

Forest or group style (YOSE-UE)

"The whispering of the leaves – the peace of the forest"

Model in nature: A wooded island, the flat rocky top of a cliff or a group of trees in an open landscape. The trees at the edge of the group have branches reaching almost to the ground on the sides facing outwards. The trees in the centre have bare stems (the branches having died due to lack of light) and flattened crowns.

Bonsai: A bonsai wood should consist of at least five trees. Following the rules of the Lo-Shu Square and the Fibonacci series, the trees should be planted at varying distances from each other and the total number of trees should be divided into separate groups. The Japanese prefer a harmonious arrangement and will only use trees of the same species. A "mixed wood" will only work if you use trees that would naturally grow together in the wild. This also means that all the trees will have the same requirements with respect to care.

Twin-trunk style (SOKAN)

"We strive towards the light out of one root"

Model in nature: Willows or alders along a stream or umbrella pines in the Mediterranean grow like this, two seeds having germinated very close to each other. As the crowns of the growing trees gradually require more and more room, the stems of the trees begin to lean outwards.

9

Formal upright style, showing a Bauhinia tomentosa.

Informal upright style, showing a Ficus benjamina.

Bonsai: This arrangement produces a very lively effect. In order to give the arrangement more artistic tension, trees should be chosen that are different in size and girth. The Japanese call these groups "man and woman" or (if the second bonsai is only marginally smaller than the first) "mother and child".

My tip: As a rule, SOKAN trees are formed out of two separate trees which are planted very close together. To make sure the two stems will nearly touch, loosen the rootstock where they meet to such an extent that the roots can be pulled out to each side. Now place the trees close together and fix them with a wire loop around both stems. Remove the wire after six months to prevent it from growing into the stem.

Formal upright style (CHOKKAN)
"Majesty"

Model in nature: If a tree grows in the middle of an open landscape and receives plenty of light from all sides, it will grow slowly and surely upwards, spreading its branches evenly in all directions and will finally turn into a splendid specimen with a magnificent crown and a huge trunk. Cattle will lie down in the shade of the spreading crown; a traveller will pause to rest.

Bonsai: In order to retain the impression of a huge tree, use a tree with a massive stem. The lower third of the stem should be kept free of branches. The ideal bowl should be of a simple, smooth shape with stable feet.

Informal upright style (MOYOGI)
"The cheerful expert in the art of living"

Model in nature: In Europe the hornbeam often takes on this shape and is a species which grows very slowly. As it copes very well with shade, it can still flourish when overtaken by faster growing neighbouring trees. The hornbeam will then continue to grow sideways, reaching out to where there is most light. In time, this results in a tree with a twisted trunk, which clearly demonstrates the tree's ability to adapt to its living conditions.

Bonsai: The stem strives towards the light in elegant curves and twists. The lowest, dominant branch appears above the first third of the entire height of the stem. The crown is positioned vertically above the trunk.

Slanting style (SHAKAN)

"I will not topple for a long time yet"
The photograph (right) shows *Ulmus parvifolia* (Japanese elm).

Model in nature: These trees are found mainly along the courses of streams and at the bottom of steep slopes. Some natural event will have caused the tree almost to topple over but not quite.

Bonsai: This shape symbolizes a tough, resilient will to survive. The lower part of the bonsai is tilted, in extreme cases it may even be lying on the ground. The top of the tree has lifted and is growing vertically. The outer parts of the branches are horizontal.

Tips on the shaping of a SHAKAN:

This shape of bonsai can be produced quite easily in a plant that has already begun to grow towards the light on one side, perhaps because it has been placed in the wrong position in the flower shop. First, replant it in a larger container so that the crown is vertical. Now the branches can be bent and held in a horizontal position with the help of bonsai wire. If necessary, you can shorten them (wiring, see p. 32; pruning, see p. 30).

Finally, place the bonsai in a well-lit position, water and fertilize it regularly and shorten the side branches, which will tend to grow too long, about every ten weeks or so.

After about six months, the crown of the plant should begin to take on the appearance of a bonsai. Now it is time to begin work on the rootstock. Remove half of the soil very carefully with a stick, cut the roots back by a third and replant the tree in a large, flat container. In another year's time, the roots will be so compact that they will need shortening again and the bonsai, which by now will have lots of branches in the crown, can be planted in its final bowl.

Slanting style (SHAKAN), showing a Japanese elm.

Broom style (HOKIDACHI), showing a Ficus benjamina.

Broom style (HOKIDACHI)

"Complete harmony in mild air"
The photograph (left) shows *Ficus benjamina*.

Model in nature: an ancient cattle pasture fringed by beech trees. These trees have broad, regularly shaped crowns, which look as though they have been trimmed along the lower edge. The round, compact crown has been shaped by wind and snow. The cattle nibble off the lower branches as high as they can reach. These beeches are an excellent example of the broom style of bonsai. Well-shaped fruit trees and trees that are typical of rain forests also demonstrate this shape.

Bonsai: The branches of the crown spread regularly outwards on all sides.

11

Semi-cascade style (HAN-KENGAI), showing a Celtis sinensis that is about 50 years old.

Semi-cascade style (HAN-KENGAI)

"A steep cliff is my home"
The photograph (above) shows *Celtis sinensis*.

Model in nature: Bushes of broom, white thorn, buckthorn or mountain pine can be found growing in this style on jutting rocks. The poor soil will not allow these trees to attain their full potential height but, if they can, they will have one branch growing out sideways into space.

Bonsai: This shape symbolizes a stubborn will to survive in spite of near starvation and inhospitable conditions. Choose a tall container for a semi-cascade and stand the bonsai on a pedestal or tall table.

My tip: Azaleas are very suitable for a semi-cascade style but not for a full cascade style.

Cascade style, showing an Ulmus parvifolia that is about 35 years old.

Cascade style (KENGAI)

"A cleft in the rock is enough to survive in"
The photograph (below) shows *Ulmus parvifolia* (Japanese elm).

Model in nature: In the southern Alps, cotoneaster bushes cling to the faces of chalk cliffs in this fashion.

Bonsai: The cascade is one of the wildest-looking styles of Japanese bonsai. The tree should be shaped in such a way that it looks as though it is forcing its roots into a crack in the rock face. The light crown hangs freely above the perilous drop; the branches reach out horizontally towards the light.

Literati style (BUNJINGI)

"Dance of a geisha in a spring breeze"
The photograph (p. 13, left) shows *Serissa foetida*.

Model in nature: In Japan there is a type of pine which grows in this shape. The nearest European equivalent is the Scots pine. Another example of this style is often seen in the fine, abstract depictions of trees in Japanese pen and ink sketches. The artists who create these lovely pictures on delicate rice paper are called "literati" in a rather clumsy translation – hence the name of this style.

Bonsai: The trees to choose for this extremely artistic style are those with very slender stems, which are planted in relatively small, round or many-sided bowls.

Root style (NEAGARI)

"Formed by the constant tides"
The photograph (p. 13, right) shows *Ficus retusa nitida* (a species of tropical fig).

Model in nature: Trees that grow naturally in this style can be found in mangrove swamps along tropical beaches; in Japan they are found along the south coast of Kyushu. A

Literati style (BUNJINGI), showing a Serissa foetida.   *Root style (NEAGARI), showing a Ficus retusa nitida.*

high tide, the tree trunks become immersed in sea water several metres deep. Often only the crown protrudes above the surface.
Bonsai: The plant must first be grown in a tall flowerpot of which only the bottom quarter contains soil. The remainder of the pot should be filled with sand.

The right bowl

The shape of the pot, its colour and the material from which it is made should all blend with the style of the bonsai. Bonsai bowls must retain their beauty for decades, so they are fired at very high temperatures and are completely impermeable to water. Specialist bonsai shops usually sell bowls imported from Japan, which are both of the right quality and aesthetically pleasing.

European-manufactured bonsai containers are cheaper but will not last as long, as they are fired at lower temperatures.

My tip: It is better to choose glazed bowls for indoor bonsai. They are less likely to form a chalky film and look better in a furnished room.

In general, flat, rectangular or oval bowls are used. The ideal measurements are that the height of the bowl should equal the diameter of the stem and the length of the bowl should equal ⅔ of the height of the tree. A bonsai with a stem 20 cm (8 in) tall would, therefore, require a bowl about 14 cm (5½ in) long.

A few tips about bowls
● If bonsai are planted in very flat

or very small bowls, each tree should be anchored in the bowl with wire (see p. 24).
● If you water plants too profusely in tall containers, waterlogging may occur. To prevent this, fill the lower third of the container with drainage material (Hortag or something similar as used in hydroculture).
● The forest or group style and the slanting style can be planted on stone slabs. Before planting, stick a "lip" made of moist clay to the edge of the stone slab to prevent the soil from being washed away when you water and to help to retain enough moisture. This creates a shallow depression which can be filled with bonsai soil for planting. The clay lip can later be hidden under a camouflage of prostrate-growing *Helxine soleirolii* or something similar.

13

Advice on buying plants and on their positioning

Indoor bonsai species originate from different climatic zones of the world and will, therefore, have rather different requirements with respect to position. Make sure that you find out about such points when choosing your plants. Just a few simple alterations in a room can improve even an unsuitable position.

The correct position

Indoor bonsai come from the warmer regions of the world, which can be roughly divided into four climatic zones:

● tropics (most *Ficus* species);
● subtropics (for example, *Serissa, Carmona*);
● Mediterranean (myrtle, pines);
● dry steppes or desert plains (all succulents).

The very different conditions found in each of these zones will determine the requirements of each individual bonsai plant in respect of its position in your home.

Before you buy any plant, check whether you will be able to provide the correct position for it and whether you can create the right conditions (for example, artificial lighting, see p. 15).

South-facing windows: During the winter, a south-facing window is ideal for all bonsai. Things are different in summer, however, when the strong midday sun hits the windowpane and can cause the plants to suffer burns. This is when you will need to provide shade, either with a blind or with a light, densely woven fabric curtain placed between the glass and the plant.

North- and east-facing windows: This is where tropical plants that like shade feel at home. However, the temperature should never be allowed to drop below 18° C (64° F).

West-facing windows: This is the ideal place for Mediterranean and subtropical plants during the summer months.

NB: You will find precise details in the instructions on caring for individual bonsai (see pp. 39-59).

Winter quarters

Some indoor bonsai, like fuchsias and pomegranates, lose their leaves in winter. If such plants are deprived of a proper period of winter dormancy, they will become sickly. If you have indoor bonsai which shed their leaves in winter, you will have to provide them with winter quarters at about 3-10° C (37-50° F).

These plants will not require light during their leafless phase, so, from early winter to the end of winter, they can be placed in a dark, cool cellar. The soil should never be allowed to dry out during this phase. From early spring onwards, bring the plants back into the light, but for at least four weeks the temperature should not be allowed to rise above 15-18° C (59-64° F).

Buying healthy plants

A healthy, well-nourished plant has deep green foliage without blemishes. Discoloration, curled-up leaf edges, sparse new shoots or a shiny film on the leaves are all indicators of infestation by pests or the symptoms of mineral deficiency (see pp. 27-9).

Seven rules when buying plants

1. Make sure the quality of the plants is excellent. If you have no experience of indoor bonsai, it is a good idea to visit a bonsai nursery (enquire at your local garden centre for addresses). Here you will find beautiful, correctly priced young plants which have been given some initial shaping by an experienced bonsai gardener and planted in an appropriate bonsai bowl.

If, however, you are intending to buy a plant in a garden centre or a flower shop, you should take special note of the following points.

2. Check whether the bonsai has been grown according to the correct rules of shaping. Low-priced bonsai, in particular, should be scrutinized with a critical eye. These cheap bonsai are often young plants that have been pruned without adherence to the rules. Correct clipping of the usually very dense, spherical crown is hardly possible for a layperson to accomplish.

3. The soil should be gritty, so that air and water can penetrate easily. Cheap bonsai have often been planted in standard potting compost, which is quite unsuitable for bonsai on account of its high peat content. This soil will have to be replaced, bit by bit, with special bonsai soil.

You may find that some well-shaped bonsai, which have been imported from China or Japan, may have been planted in clay in their country of origin. Water cannot permeate the clay and the roots will end up being suffocated. The clay will have to be exchanged for bonsai soil in two or three gradual stages.

4. Make sure the bonsai is sitting firmly in the soil.

5. The plant should have unblemished foliage and healthy new shoots.

6. The bonsai should be growing in a bowl that complements the shape of the tree and is made of very hard material that was fired at high temperatures (see p. 13).

7. Finally, make sure that you are indeed buying an indoor bonsai and not an outdoor one (several species of indoor bonsai are described on pp. 39-59).

More light in dark corners

If you want to stand your bonsai in the centre of the room or against an indoor wall, you will require a source of artificial light of sufficient wattage to maintain good health. A wide range of plant lamps can be obtained in the gardening trade. Which one you choose will depend on personal taste and the amount of money you wish to spend.

Plants require bright, slightly yellow light for twelve to fourteen hours a day to remain healthy. After a maximum of four weeks, you will be able to tell if the light is sufficient. If the new shoots are dark green, all is well. Light green, lanky new shoots are an unmistakable sign of lack of light.

Mercury arc, halogen quartz or iodine quartz lamps: These hanging lamps are particularly suitable for solitary plants but are relatively expensive. They create very bright light from a low consumption of electricity.

Fluorescent tube lighting: These tubes are a cheap alternative.

A plant lamp will create the right conditions in a dark position.

15

Combinations of a tube of daylight white with a warm colour tube, or even one white and two warm tones, are ideal. These lamps are suitable for lighting up a corner niche, a display cabinet or a windowsill that does not receive much light.
NB: Mercury arc lamps, halogen quartz and iodine quartz lamps and fluorescent tubes should be discarded with special waste rather than ordinary household rubbish.
A time switch is very useful for regulating the hours of light: Plants have a very precise growth cycle. This means that any additional lighting should be switched on and off at the same time every day.

Raising the humidity
Many indoor bonsai find the very arid air that occurs indoors during the winter months difficult to cope with. The traditional indoor bonsai, for example *Sageretia*, *Serissa* and *Carmona*, which originate from the subtropical coastal regions of China and Japan, are much affected by this but there are ways of alleviating the problem.
A tray of gravel: Stand your bonsai on very large waterproof trays filled with lime-free gravel or Hortag etc. Keep the gravel moist at all times. As the water evaporates, it will create a better climate around the plants.
A bonsai terrarium: If the bonsai are kept in a semi-closed or completely closed space, much higher humidity can be attained. A glass aquarium or goldfish bowl may be sufficient for a small bonsai. If you have several tropical bonsai, you can ask a glazier to make you a terrarium that opens at the front. A closed glass display case is also ideal. On top of the case you can install a high output aquarium lamp to provide additional lighting.

Caring for bonsai

Like all indoor plants, bonsai have very individual requirements in regard to care. Like most house plants, they have to be watered, fertilized and repotted but in some ways they are rather different from other green indoor plants because they require special soil, are always put back in the same bowl when they are repotted and you will have to develop some sensitivity when watering and fertilizing.

Daily observation
The secret of successful indoor gardening is to keep a careful eye on the plants in order to recognize the delicate signals they use to indicate their state of health. Bonsai are normal plants in all respects. They have not been bred through dwarfism, which would make them delicate plants that are susceptible to all kinds of problems. Nor are they starved or crippled, which would make them particularly susceptible to disease and in need of lots of special care.
The leaves or needles are the most obvious indicators of problems. Their colours can vary from lush green ("I feel fine") to pale green ("I'm not feeling so good") to blackish-green ("I feel really ill").
The attitude of the leaves and needles also indicates the plant's condition: a plant bursting with health will have leaves that stand out firmly on the branches. The first, unmistakable signs of lack of care or the beginnings of illness are leaves that hang limply. In the case of conifers, the needles will be slightly bent.
You should spend at least five seconds a day studying each bonsai. This will be sufficient to check its state of health.
● Has the colour of the leaves changed from dark to pale green?
● Do the leaves (or needles) look healthy and firm on their branches?
● Are there any blemishes or discoloration of leaves or branches (infestation with pests)?
● Is the soil dry or slightly moist?

After this little observation, you can decide whether to reach for the watering can, fertilizer bottle or plant protection agents.

The most important tools for working with bonsai.

The right tools

Over the last thousand years, Japanese and Chinese bonsai gardeners have developed certain specialist techniques and tools for use with bonsai.

The flat, waterproof planting bowls have large drainage holes which are covered with small grids (see p. 23). There are special tools for pruning twigs and branches: well-sharpened scissors for a clean cut and pincers with very sharp blades for removing branches at the stem. A metal hook on a pointed stick is used to loosen the dense root system. Long-necked watering cans, with spouts that produce the finest shower of water, have also been developed, but these can only be used outside. There are special pliers for cutting and bending bonsai wire.

My tip: Use the root hook very carefully to avoid damaging any of the roots.

The tools in the photographs above are:

1. Top row: wire pliers for uncoiling wire; a wire cutter for snipping off lengths of wire; bonsai scissors for pruning branches and twigs.
Bottom row: concave pliers for removing branches close to the stem; small bonsai scissors for the finest twigs; a leaf cutter; tweezers for plucking out the finest shoots.
2. Small hand brush for smoothing the soil.
3. Root hook for loosening and removing used up soil.

1. First, moisten the dried soil with a plant mister. Water from an ordinary watering can would just run off the soil's surface.

2. The moistened surface will now absorb water quite readily.

How to water bonsai

1. **First moisten the soil:** A bonsai should not be watered straightaway with an ordinary watering can because the soil is heaped up in a small mound in the bowl to create the effect of a section cut out of a landscape. This mound would cause the water to run off the soil without moistening it, so it will have to be moistened first with a mister or plant spray.

2. **Next, use an ordinary watering can** as the water will now be able to penetrate the pre-moistened soil.

3. **Using a bonsai watering can:** This type of can has a "shower" attachment with extremely fine holes, which can rapidly moisten a very dry soil surface. Water until surplus water flows out of the drainage holes in the bottom of the bowl. Watering in this way will always cause a slight flood, so it can only be done outside (or in a bathtub).

Complete submersion during a drought

If a bonsai has become rather dried out, it can be placed in a container of water for several hours. The water should not, however, reach over the edge of the bowl. Give your bonsai a "bath" about every ten days.

This specially designed bonsai watering can is only suitable for outside us

Watering by means of a wick

This device will make watering considerably easier. The bonsai are placed on water-filled trays and suck up the required moisture through wicks.

You will need:
● a large crochet needle for drawing the wick through the drainage holes;
● a plaited cord;
● watertight, flat trays that complement the colour and size of the bonsai;
● Hortag or lime-free gravel of the type used in aquariums.

Method
1. Cut some lengths of cord (40 cm/16 in) to use as wicks. Push the crochet needle down through a drainage hole from above, hook the cord around it and pull the cord up through the soil.
2. Pull a cord up through each of the drainage holes.
3. Stand the bonsai bowl on a gravel-filled tray. The bonsai itself should not be standing in water! Press the wicks into the gravel and fill the tray with water.

Do not keep the bonsai too wet: This very useful method of watering can sometimes cause the bonsai to become waterlogged. You should never water immediately the tray is empty of water but should wait until the surface of the soil in the bowl is dry.

Watering while you are away from home: If you use this method to water your bonsai, you will only need to replenish the water about every eight to ten days. If you stand them in a large tub filled with moist peat, they will be fine for up to three weeks.

My tip: Before you actually go away, test how long a particular quantity of water will last.

1. A wick made of cord is hooked around a large crochet needle.

2. The wick should protrude about 20 cm (8 in) from the drainage hole.

3. The bonsai is placed on a tray filled with gravel.

When to water

You can easily tell whether it is time to water your bonsai by checking with a finger.

The general rule is: if the surface of the soil is moist, do not water; if it is almost dry, water.

NB: If a pot plant is kept wet all the time, its roots will rot and it will die. So, although the soil should not be allowed to dry out completely, neither should it be watered too often.

The right water

Many indoor bonsai originate from regions with almost lime-free humus soils. This includes all tropical trees (e.g. *Ficus*) and the azaleas (*Rhododendron*). If such plants are given hard water they will soon suffer from chlorosis (see photograph, p. 28).

To find out how hard your mains water is, ask your local water authority. If this value is below 13 degrees Clark you need not worry about using mains water for your bonsai. *Ficus* and *Rhododendron* species should be replanted in new soil every year, using soil that contains peat.

If the hardness value of your water falls between 13-19 degrees Clark, boiling the water before use will reduce the alkaline content. As boiling also drives out oxygen, you should allow the water to stand in a flat container for some hours after boiling.

Very hard water should always be measured: Hard water, of a value above 19 degrees Clark, should always be treated before using it for bonsai plants. Measure the acidity (pH value) and degree of hardness before and after treating the water. You should be able to obtain all the necessary agents and gadgets for treating and testing water at an aquarium suppliers.

● The acidity value should always be pH 6.5 to 7.0.

● The total hardness should always be below 19 degrees Clark.

Mixing mains water with rainwater: Rainwater is soft but can be quite acid (up to pH 3). Start by gradually mixing 1 litre (1¾ pt) of mains water with rainwater until your measurements yield favourable values. Then use the same ratio to mix the water you want to use for watering your bonsai.

Using peat to soften your water: Hang a linen bag filled with peat in your plant water-storage container. After one to two days, the acid in the peat will have neutralized the lime in the water. The peat will need to be exchanged every few weeks.

Buying water-softening agents: The gardening trade offers a range of plant-friendly softening agents. Tables giving the correct mixing ratios for various degrees of hardness should appear on the packaging.

NB: Never use softening agents intended for kettles, kitchen gadgets, etc. These agents contain mixtures of different acids or soda and both are harmful to plants. Never use water derived from a softening device that utilizes salt (sodium chloride) for the process. Water that has been softened by an ion-exchange device is also unsuitable for plants as it is usually too acid.

Fertilizing

Bonsai grow in relatively small amounts of soil, which should also contain correspondingly small amounts of controlled-release fertilizer. Your bonsai will, therefore, require regular doses of liquid fertilizer.

Liquid fertilizers are suitable for all bonsai which are, after all, ordinary trees that grow, flower and sometimes even bear fruit. Compound fertilizers contain all the required nutrients and trace elements in the correct ratios. Liquid fertilizers, which are given in water, are best. As so little soil is present, solid or powdered fertilizers could easily lead to burning of the roots.

Organic bonsai liquid fertilizer: Through the specialist gardening trade you will be able to obtain liquid organic fertilizers that have been formulated specially for bonsai. The concentration of nutrients and trace elements contained in these is tailored to suit the small amounts of soil used for growing bonsai.

Tips on fertilizing

1. Use only liquid fertilizers for indoor bonsai.
2. If using ordinary fertilizers for bonsai, use only half of the recommended concentration.
3. During the summer months, indoor bonsai should receive a dose of fertilizer every two to three weeks; during the winter months this should be given every four to six weeks.
4. These times should be doubled for old, slow-growing bonsai.

Repotting

With very few exceptions (see instructions on care, pp. 39-59), indoor bonsai do not really have a rest period, so they can be repotted at almost any time of the year. Unlike other house plants, bonsai will remain in the same container for decades – only the soil should be renewed. The container and its plant should have measurements that correspond to certain ratios (see p. 13). If the tree has grown a lot, however, then it should be repotted in a suitable, larger bowl.

A charming decoration

This massive bonsai (Ficus retusa crassifolia) has been teamed with African violets in a similarly shaped bonsai bowl.

1. The soil is thick with fibrous roots – high time to replant.

2. Remove one third of the soil with a pointed stick.

3. The roots no longer seem to fit in their previous container.

Fibrous roots which have grown too long can be shortened quite easily.

First steps when repotting

1. If the bonsai has been growing in the same soil for about a year, lift it out of its bowl carefully and check whether a densely matted root system has formed around the edges of the bowl – if so, it is time to repot it. If the rootstock has grown so much that it is visibly lifting the bonsai out of its bowl, then it is certainly time to replant it!
Allow the soil to become a bit drier than usual before repotting, as this will make it easier to remove the old soil from the roots.

2. After removing the bonsai from its bowl, clean the bowl with an old brush or a dry cloth. Remove one third to half – no more! – of the old soil with your fingertips or a pointed stick.

3. Hold the plant in its bowl and spread the roots out flat and sideways.

4. Finally, cut off enough root so that there is a finger's width of space between the edge of the bowl and the rootstock. If there is no drainage grid over the hole, now is the time to insert one in the bowl

How to fix a drainage grid

A small drainage grid should be inserted over each drainage hole in the bonsai bowl. These small devices can be obtained through the specialist bonsai trade.

1. The drainage grids are fixed in the bowl with wire, as shown in the photographs. Wire that is 1-2 mm thick is suitable.
2. Draw the wire loops through the grid.
3. Bend the loops over so that the grid becomes firmly fixed in the hole.

Tips when repotting

● If your bonsai displays sickly growth, for example, if it is producing only small, light-coloured leaves, this usually means that the soil is exhausted.

● Young trees which are expected to grow larger should be repotted every year. About every two years, they should be replanted in a pot with a diameter that is a few centimetres larger than the previous one.

● Older trees which have attained their final shape should be repotted only every two to three years. They should only need to be replanted in a new container every few decades.

● Leave a freshly wired bonsai for at least eight weeks before replanting it, and do not alter the direction of branches by wiring immediately after replanting a tree.

NB: A pot plant cannot flourish if kept in the same pot with the same soil for many years. Waste material from the roots will accumulate in the confines of the pot. After some time, the plant will also have used up the humus in the soil and this means that there will be no nutrients left and the plant container will be filled with a densely matted root system. As a rule, bonsai which have only a little soil in their bowls need repotting every one to two years.

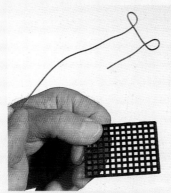

1. A small grid for covering a drainage hole.

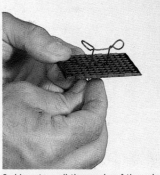

2. How to pull the ends of the wire loops through the small grid.

3. The ends of the wire are poked through the hole and bent over.

The right soil

Bonsai bowls are shallow and their walls are not porous. Bonsai soil should be of a grainy consistency so that water can penetrate easily. A good bonsai soil should contain the following ingredients:

● humus to promote the growth of the roots;

● porous, coarse sand (of a diameter up to 4 mm), which will absorb water easily and also store it;

● clay, which will store water and prevent nutrients from being washed out;

● peat to neutralize the lime in hard water.

Suitable soils

Special bonsai soil can be bought in the gardening trade. However, a mixture that will prove quite suitable for the very special requirements of your bonsai can be made up at home. You should be able to obtain all the necessary ingredients in the gardening trade.

Nearly all indoor bonsai will thrive on the following mixture:
3 parts standard soil containing peat and loam;
2 parts fine bark humus (particles up to 8 mm in diameter);
2 parts pumice or lava sand (grains up to 5 mm in diameter).

Tropical trees (all *Ficus* species), azaleas and fuchsias require slightly acid soil:
3 parts standard compost;
2 parts seedling compost or ericaceous compost suitable for azaleas;
1 part fine bark humus (particles up to 8 mm in diameter);
2 parts pumice or lava sand.

Plants from steppes or dry desert plains will require plenty of sand:
2 parts standard compost;
2 parts fine bark humus;
2 parts pumice or lava sand.

1. Hold the plant firmly with one hand while filling the bowl with soil.

2. A wire goes across the roots and down through the hole.

How to replant a bonsai

1. After you have inserted a small grid over each drainage hole in the bowl and fixed each one with wire, put a thin layer of soil in the bowl. Set the bonsai plant on top of this and move it into the right position.

2. Fix the plant in place with a piece of wire about 2-4 mm thick. Push the wire up through the drainage hole in the bottom of the bowl and make a loop to prevent it from slipping through.

3. Holding the bonsai in the desired position, pull the wire taut and then twist it around the stem. Now pile up soil until the roots are well covered all the way round.

My tip: A pot plant that you are training as a bonsai will often have roots that have grown crookedly, caused by the narrow confines of the bowl. Do not cut off these roots but incorporate them in the "design" by placing a stone underneath them to lift them up.

3. Pull the end of the wire taut and wrap it around the stem.

4. A free-standing root lying across a stone looks very natural.

4. Using your fingertips or a pencil-thick, pointed stick, press the soil well down between the roots and add more soil if necessary. Make sure the tops of the roots remain uncovered, just like the roots of a tree in the wild. Place a stone underneath the roots to make them look more natural.

5. Surplus soil can be removed quite easily with a small hand brush.

6. Stand the freshly planted bonsai bowl in a dish and fill this with water but do not allow the water to come up over the edge of the bonsai bowl. Leave the bonsai to stand in the water until the surface of the soil is quite moist (this will take several hours).

Care after repotting

A large proportion of the fine, fibrous roots which normally supply the plant with water will have been

5. Remove surplus soil from on top of the roots with a small hand brush.

removed in cutting back the root-stock. The renewed growth of these fine roots will take two to three weeks. During this period, the indoor bonsai should be given a semi-shady, reasonably warm position and watered very carefully. The soil should not be allowed to dry out nor should it be so wet that the roots start to decay. After replanting, the bonsai should not be fertilized again for six to eight weeks.

My tip: The bare surface of the soil of a freshly replanted bonsai does not look very natural. If grown outside or in the moist atmosphere of a greenhouse, small mosses will tend to grow on the soil quite naturally. In the case of indoor bonsai, under-planting with ground-covering plants will look very attractive. *Helxine soleirolii* and *Sagina subulata* (star moss) are very suitable. An accompanying plant, growing in a container that complements the bonsai bowl, can be very effective (see p. 21). The bonsai and accompanying plant should both originate from similar climates so that they will harmonize and share the same needs for care.

The freshly planted bonsai is watered in a flat dish.

Pests and diseases

You will only be able to control pests and diseases if you can identify them and know what causes them. Many pests can be controlled with agents that are harmless to people. The use of dangerous chemicals should be left entirely to experts.

Animal pests

Not all pests that suck a plant's sap are insects. The animal pests that prey on decorative plants come from two groups: insects and mites. In order to control them effectively, you need to understand that the bodily functions of these two groups are rather different. Insects will drown in soapy water but mites will survive for days. On the other hand, the skin of tiny mites is so delicate that ordinary ethyl alcohol is lethal to them in concentrations that would be quite harmless for humans. Harmful fungi, particularly mildew and grey mould, can also infest indoor bonsai. Fungi only feel comfortable in a damp climate, so they rarely appear indoors. An infestation by fungi will only become a problem if you have a large collection of plants in a greenhouse or keep sensitive plants in a sealed glass case during the winter.

Controlling pests without toxins

Indoors, as a rule, you should always begin by using pest control substances that are harmless to people. Only if these means fail should one resort to more severe methods. You should always leave the use of toxic plant protection agents to experts. This involves taking an infested indoor bonsai to a specialist gardener whom you trust. *If you do decide to use a toxic plant spray yourself, please ensure that you observe the following precautions:*

● Make sure that you seek advice from an expert beforehand.
● Never use toxic plant sprays in enclosed areas. Always take the infested plant outside for treatment, or into a separate room (shed, garage, etc.), where no food intended for human or animal consumption is stored, and which can be properly aired afterwards.
● Protect your skin with rubber gloves.
NB: Most of the following methods and agents are harmless to people (any exceptions are mentioned) but proper handling of these agents and solutions is still necessary. Please make absolutely sure that children and pets are unable to gain access to any of these agents.

Derris-pyrethrum

Derris is a woody, climbing, tropical plant with a root that contains rotenone, a substance toxic to fish and insects. Pyrethrum is the old name for two *Chrysanthemum* species from Asia Minor and North Africa, both of which contain insect toxins (pyrethrine) in their flowers. Rotenone and pyrethrine are considered to be non-toxic to humans (see Warning below). You can obtain mixtures containing these substances in the gardening trade. They are used to control aphids.

Warning: These substances are considered to be non-toxic to humans as they are not easily absorbed through the mouth or skin. According to most recent findings, however, they are extremely toxic if they reach the human nervous system directly through the blood stream. This means that you must take care if you have an injury or skin disease, especially if you suffer from allergies! Spray only when you are wearing gloves and when there is no wind. Insecticides containing pyrethroids are even more dangerous. This substance is a synthetically produced version of pyrethrum.

An attractive grouping of cypresses
This group style arrangement of Cupressus macrocarpa (Californian cypress) is 60 cm (24 in) tall. It was shaped by the author from 2 m (80 in) tall large container plants.

Soap solution

Soap and washing up liquids are non-toxic but, even so, you can combat insect pests with these rather ordinary substances by drowning them in a solution. Insects will not drown in ordinary water. Because their chitinous body armour does not absorb water, their bodies become enveloped in a kind of air bubble if they fall into clear water. If a little kitchen soap, liquid soap or washing up liquid is introduced to the water, it is then able to penetrate the fine tracheae (through which the insects breathe) and they drown.

Method

Fill a large bucket right to the top with water and dissolve a little soap or two to three squirts of washing up liquid in it. Lay two long wooden spoons, a coat hanger or something similar across the top of the bucket, then dip the infested bonsai plant, head down, in the solution. The roots should not come into contact with the soap solution, so they should be supported on the wooden spoons or coat hanger. The crown of the little tree may be left in the solution for two to three hours. Finally, remove the bonsai from the solution and allow it to drip. Next day, spray the bonsai with clear water.

Repeat this procedure two to three times at intervals of five days.

Use to combat insects.

My tip: Aphids can also be controlled by spraying them with a 1% liquid soap solution (the leaves should be wet).

Aphids

These are green or black insects the size of a pinhead. Winged and wingless types often appear together. The first signs are a shiny-sticky substance on the leaves (honeydew, see photograph).

Control: soap solution (spraying or drowning), spray with alcohol or insecticides.

Mealy bugs

The first signs of infestation are cotton-wool-like waxy secretions in the forks of twigs. The young insects are hidden in this substance. Adult mealy bugs are flattish, light pink Insects up to 5 mm long.

Control: drowning in a soap solution or watering with systemic insecticides.

Scale insects

Only the tiny (0.3 mm) larvae and the equally tiny male insects move about. The mature females appear as brown, fixed "scabs" on the leaves and twigs. Again, the first sign of their presence is honeydew on the leaves.

Control: drowning in soap solution, watering with systemic insecticides.

Chlorosis

Caused by a mineral deficiency, which occurs in *Ficus* and azalea species if the water is too hard. As a prevention, use soil containing plenty of peat and softened water.

Control: 0.5 g of iron sulphate in 1 litre (1¾ pt) of water. The sick plant should be watered several times with this solution and repotted in soil containing peat.

White fly

The larvae are 1 mm long, green and motionless. Mature insects resemble minute white butterflies. If you touch the plant, they fly up in a small cloud. First symptoms: honeydew on the leaves.
Control: drowning in soap solution, watering with systemic insecticides.

Mildew

This is caused by a fungus. The fungus forms a white bloom on the leaves, making them look as though they have been dusted with flour. Prevention is achieved by making sure the air is drier. Avoid spraying the plants with water.
Control: spraying with mare's tail brew, water glass or fungicides.

Red spider mites

These minute (0.1-0.3 mm long) mites are difficult to see even with the help of a magnifying glass. A symptom of infestation is the spotty discoloration of the leaves.
Control: spraying with 25% ethyl alcohol or an acaricide. Unfortunately, most insecticides are ineffective against red spider mites.

Water glass

This can be obtained from most chemists.
Method
First prepare a concentration as described on the packaging.
Then dilute a small amount of this in water in a ratio of one part to ten parts of water and spray the infested plants. Store it out of the reach of children, in a clean bottle labelled "water glass" to prevent accidents – water glass is not drinkable!
Using a measuring jug or beaker, pour 100 ml (4 fl oz) of the original solution into the bottle and then make this up to 1 litre (1¾ pt) with water.
Use against mildew and grey mould.

Mare's tail brew

(Hippuris vulgaris)
This brew is an old and well-tested recipe for controlling mildew and grey mould if it is used early enough.
Method
Boil a good handful of dried mare's tail in water for three to five minutes and then allow this concoction to cool. Now filter it through a coffee filter.
Spray any plants that are infested with fungi with the undiluted liquid. After this treatment, stand the bonsai in a bright position but not in direct sunlight.
Use against mildew and grey mould.

Alcohol

Ethyl-alcohol is highly toxic to cellular tissue, so plants cannot be sprayed with pure alcohol as the leaves would be destroyed. Use a solution of one part spirit to three parts water.
Method
Spray the infested parts of the plant with the solution, taking special care to spray the undersides of the leaves as this is where the pests like to congregate.
Allow the alcohol time to work (if necessary cover the bonsai with plastic film).
After about an hour, spray the plant with clear water.
This procedure should be repeated three times at intervals of three to five days.
Use against insects and mites.

My tip: If you add a few squirts of washing up liquid, the solution will even penetrate the wax or chitinous body armour of mealy bugs and scale insects.

Training bonsai

The different styles of bonsai are copied from the shapes of trees in the wild and the bonsai will have to be reshaped from time to time if it is to retain its special "look". Pruning and wiring are the main ways of retaining a particular shape or of improving it. How to do this is explained in this chapter.

The various species of indoor bonsai grow at different rates. Some, for example, *Ulmus parvifolia*, have to be pruned three or four times a year. On the other hand, *Ficus retusa crassifolia* and some of the succulents grow so slowly that cutting back is only necessary every second year.

The time comes when every bonsai needs to be shaped so that its original beauty is not lost. Indoor bonsai can be pruned at any time of year. The best time, however, is probably from the first to the second month of spring.

The basic rules of pruning

The following information should enable you to carry out the fascinating business of pruning yourself. However, if you still lack the courage to cut your own much loved plant, any good bonsai nursery will undertake pruning or reshaping procedures for you. Most bonsai nurseries also offer regular courses in this art. You may also be fortunate enough to live near to a bonsai club (see p. 60), where bonsai enthusiasts meet regularly. If you contact such a club, you should find that its members will be only too happy to give you advice or help.

My tip: Do not try out your pruning skills for the first time on your most valuable specimen. Indoor azaleas make reasonably priced "guinea pigs" for practising on. These small shrubs are quite easy to convert to a broom style (HOKIDACHI) by thinning out branches that are too close together and pruning the flat crown sideways.

The most important point about pruning any bonsai is to take your time to study the plant and think about what you are doing – do not just grab the scissors and snip!

In general, when pruning remember that:

● The crown grows vertically upwards.
● The lateral branches stand out flat and sideways.
● The front of the bonsai should be left open so that you can see most of the stem and the branches.
● Only the back of the crown is left closed.
● The position of the buds will determine the direction of growth. Every leaf axil will have a bud. After pruning, it is the first two or three buds on a branch that will produce shoots.

If the leaf is situated underneath the branch, the new shoot will grow straight towards you. If the leaf is positioned sideways, the new shoot will grow in that direction.

If the leaf is on top of the branch, the shoot will grow vertically upwards.

● Immediately after cutting back, the crown should look a little "slimmer" than the ideal picture of a bonsai.
● Pruning the tree is quite a shock to the plant's system, so do not keep snipping away at your bonsai but leave it to recuperate for at least eight weeks after each pruning session.

My tip: *Ficus* and *Euphorbia* species contain a milky sap which oozes out of any cuts or injuries. This sap will curdle in water or in temperatures above 60° C (140° F). Spray clear water on the plant after cutting. The sap from larger cuts can be made to set by holding the flame of a cigarette lighter near to it (for the maximum of one second!).

1. The shape of the crown can no longer be seen – high time for pruning.

2. Shoots growing upwards from the branch are cut back to one to three leaves.

How to prune

1. Spend some time having a good look at your tree and deciding which branch should be the one to form the crown shoot. This branch should be the strongest one and should be more or less vertical. Then make a decision about the future height of your bonsai and shorten this crown shoot so that only three to five leaves or buds are left above the last fork. The most recent bud should be pointing upwards.

2. Now begin to form the silhouette of the new crown, pruning the crown (just as you would a garden shrub) into an irregular cone shape. The lateral branches will now be about the right length, so you can prune them so that they take on a triangular shape if you look at them from above. While you are doing this, make sure that the foremost leaf is situated on the lower edge of each branch. The buds at the shoot tips will grow laterally.

Any lateral branches that are growing vertically upwards should be cut back to one to three leaves which will later give a cushion-like effect. If two larger branches are so close together that they are still not clearly separate after being cut back, it is better to remove the one that will create the smaller gap in the general appearance of the tree (unless this effect is the one you want).

Any cuts that are wider than the diameter of a pencil should be sealed with a disinfecting substance.

3. The structure of the crown will now be clearly visible. Each individual branch should be free-standing, without touching its neighbour. The frontal view of the crown should appear relatively flat, as no branch should be growing directly towards the observer.

The back of the tree should be denser and broader, as the branches will jut out quite a bit beyond the edge of the bowl.

After pruning. The arrangement of the branches is clearly visible again.

1. *Wind the wire two or three times around the stem.*

2. *Two branches, reinforced with one wire, support each other.*

3. *The stem is gently turned through 180 degrees.*

4. *Now the top branch is turned in exactly the opposite direction.*

A beginner's course in wiring

Wiring is used to correct the direction of growth of an individual branch. If, for example, a branch is growing too close to another, or if the crown has a gap which could be closed by a neighbouring branch, this problem can be corrected by wiring. Choose the branch you wish to alter, wind a thick wire around it and then gently bend it in the desired direction. (The photographs show how this is done.)

5. *A practice branch has been wired in the informal upright style (MOYOG*

First steps in the art of bonsai

Your very own bonsai, which you have grown, shaped and trained from an ordinary pot plant during the course of several years, is the crowning achievement of this fascinating hobby. Start with inexpensive, easy-to-care-for types of woody plants which grow willingly. The first steps are shown here using a *Ficus benjamina* and an indoor azalea to demonstrate how to create a bonsai out of a young tree that will eventually end up looking old and venerable.

1. The wire (either covered with a copper sheath or brown, anodized, aluminium wire) should be about a third of the thickness of the branch. Start with two or three twists around the stem to stabilize the arrangement. Then draw the wire up through the first fork and wind it in shallow spirals (at an angle of 45 degrees) around the branch. Make sure you do not squash any leaves or lateral branches.

2. The same piece of wire can be used to support two branches. Wind the centre of the piece of wire around the stem for two or three twists, then wind the ends around the two branches.

3. Now grip the stem with both hands and gently turn it in the desired direction.

4. Next, the arrangement of the branches can be corrected. All lateral branches should grow towards the outside from a bend in the main part of the branch.

5. Wind several parallel wires around the stem and the branches. In a few months' time, even if you remove a piece of wire rather too late, it will still not be able to "strangle" the wood if the wires are lying parallel. If you have accidentally crossed two wires when winding them, there is a risk of the branch dying off. Remove the wire after about six months, by cutting it up with sharp, side-cutting pliers. If you leave the wire on for too long, it will create ugly scars on the bark.

Further tips on wiring

Practise wiring a few discarded branches before trying it for real.

If a branch is growing horizontally in the wrong direction, it would be better to turn the stem rather than bend the branch around the stem.

The general direction of the branch should only be changed very slightly. A good bonsai looks natural not tortured!

You will get a good introduction to the really artistic side of this hobby by shaping ordinary pot plants into bonsai. If you do not have much patience and wish to have a tree that you can show off within two or three years, you should not bother with seeds or cuttings. It is simpler and quicker to start off with fairly large pot plants that branch out well at the stem.

From normal pot plant to indoor bonsai

Suitable pot plants: Pot plants that grow fast are recommended for beginners. They should branch well and be easy to care for. I recommend the following plants for your first attempts at shaping:
● indoor azalea (*Rhododendron japonicum*);
● myrtle (*Myrtus communis*);
● thyme (*Thymus vulgaris*);
● rosemary (*Rosmarinus officinalis*);
● elm (*Ulmus parvifolia*);
● sageretia (*Sageretia thea*);
● all tropical species of *Ficus*.

Sources: Thyme and rosemary can be obtained in many garden centres and nurseries in the section selling culinary herbs. Myrtle can also often be found in such places. The other species mentioned above can be obtained through specialist bonsai mail order outlets (enquire at your local garden centre).

Choice of plants: When you are choosing plants in a garden centre or tree nursery, make sure that they have lots of branches, particularly lower down. Try to imagine what the future crown of the tree will look like after you have shaped this out of the lowest three to eight branches of the original tree.

Tips on shaping: The shape of the original plant will determine the style you go for. Do not try to force your plant into a particular style and shape but allow yourself to be guided by its own natural shape of growth. The most important criterion for a good bonsai is not "In which style is my tree shaped?" but "Could my bonsai pass for a normal tree in the wild if it were larger?"

1. A 1 m (40 in) Ficus benjamina is shortened to about 35 cm (14 in).

2. After cutting, the lower branches are allowed to remain longer.

Shaping a *Ficus benjamina* into a bonsai

I chose a *Ficus benjamina* that was almost 1 m (40 in) tall for this demonstration. The stem is about as thick as a human finger. The plant will be shaped into the rather severe formal upright style (CHOKKAN).

1. First shorten the *Ficus* by about two thirds.

2. Seven branches remain. The stem of the original 1-m (40 in) plant now looks relatively strong and knobbly at a height of 35 cm (14 in).

My tip: *Ficus* trees contain a milky sap which will rapidly curdle if it comes into contact with water. Leave a piece of branch uncut beyond the last leaf or on the crown branch. Wait until the youngest bud has unfolded before removing this end piece of branch, so that the tree is not at risk of damage.

The basic shape of CHOKKAN is a pyramid, so the remaining branches are shortened to create a pyramid silhouette.

3. The branches are wrapped in bonsai wire and then bent into a horizontal position. This corresponds to the positions of the branches of a very old tree and encourages bud development. The topmost branch of the truncated tree should be bent after wiring so that it continues to grow straight upwards. At the site of the first bud it should be bent horizontally.

Transplanting the bonsai from a flowerpot to a bonsai bowl

Whenever branches are forced into a new direction of growth by means of bonsai wire, the flow of sap within them is disrupted, so do not cut back the root system at the same time. Moving the plant to a bonsai bowl should be left for another six months.

3. This Ficus benjamina has attained the basic shape of a slender pyramid.

1. The large rootstock should have enough room in this bonsai bowl.

2. Once freed of loose soil, the roots appear relatively small.

3. The main root is shortened. The sap thickens in contact with water.

Place the bonsai in a bright position and water and fertilize it regularly until the plant is ready for the next step. Two to three weeks after the first shaping procedure, the buds will begin to form and six months later the rather bare branches will be covered with new growth. Now the plant can be cut back and planted in a bonsai bowl.

. Choose a bonsai bowl with a length or diameter that is at least two thirds of the height of the tree.
. Lift the rootstock out of the pot and gently remove the loose soil.
. Shorten the central tap root and the ends of the fibrous roots to a length at which they will fit comfortably into the bonsai bowl.
. Now plant the tree in the new bowl in soil containing peat. Regular pruning and occasional wiring will gradually produce a proper bonsai. The new shoots should be cut back two to four times a year. Upright branches should be shaped with wire. In about two to three years' time you will have an attractive young bonsai.

4. After one and a half years, the shape is gradually beginning to appear.

1. The original plant used for a semi-cascade style – an azalea pyramid.

A bonsai in two hours!

Indoor azaleas are generally pruned several times before they are sold. For this reason, these small shrubs tend to have lots of branches and it is a relatively easy matter to shape a well-grown azalea into the broom style (HOKIDACHI) (see p. 11). Here, I shall demonstrate the development of a semi-cascade (HAN-KENGAI, see p. 12), from a pyramid-shaped azalea:

1. For this style, choose a plant with longish shoots and plenty of branches on one side. Choose a bonsai bowl that is fairly tall (known as a KENGAI bowl) and which is wide enough for the rootstock to fit comfortably. As you are going to wire the plant, the root must not be interfered with. The side of the plant with less branches will be turned into the underside of the semi-cascade. Remove all branches that would grow vertically downwards in the new arrangement.

2. Very carefully, remove the topmost layer of soil that is free of roots.

3. Azalea wood is rather brittle and breaks easily. Be careful to bend the stem into very gentle curves and support it with your thumbs while you are doing so.

2. The lower part of the stem is carefully freed of soil without damaging the roots.

3. Azalea wood is brittle. While bending the stem, support it firmly with both thumbs.

4. The cut azalea is planted at a slant in a tall container.

5. The stem is wired and shaped.

4. Plant the bonsai at an angle in its bowl. Take a thick piece of bonsai wire, with one end twisted into a flat loop, and push it through a drainage hole and up through the rootstock so that it protrudes out of the soil as close as possible to the stem. The wire should be about one third of the thickness of the stem and one third longer than the length of the bowl and the azalea put together.

5. Wind this wire around the stem of the azalea right to the tip and then bend the stem into the elegant curve of the semi-cascade style. Now reinforce all the lateral branch-es with thinner wire, and also short-en them if necessary. The branches should be bent into a position that will make all the shoot tips point "towards the light out of the cleft in the rock".

6. The branches of the tree should spread as far as possible and the main stem should look curved when viewed from above.

Tips on shaping azaleas

If the following basic rules are observed, azaleas should produce plenty of shoots.

● Make sure you always leave at least one leaf when pruning so that the flow of sap is assured.

● Pull a transparent plastic bag loosely over the rigorously pruned bush. The higher humidity inside the bag will prevent the cut branches from drying out too much.

● Azaleas are not suitable for two of the classical bonsai styles: the root style (NEAGARI) and the cas-cade (KENGAI). Their roots are not tough enough and are too compact for the NEAGARI style, while the flow of sap is relatively meagre, which usually results in loss of sap to the downward-hanging shoots of a KENGAI, so that the tip of the bonsai will wither and die.

The finished semi-cascade style. The stem bends downwards and the lateral branches spread upwards.

A selection of beautiful indoor bonsai

The following pages introduce a selection of the most popular indoor bonsai, together with colour photographs and detailed instructions on care. The plants have been grouped according to the climatic zones in their countries of origin, which means that they share similar requirements for care. The groupings cover Mediterranean countries, subtropical areas, tropical areas and dry desert plains or steppes. The palms form a separate group.

Explanation of keywords

At the beginning, you will always find the scientific name and, if possible, the English common name.
Origin: will give you some idea of the requirements of the plant.
Care: will give an indication as to whether the plant might be suitable for a beginner.
Position: will give information on requirements for light and temperature and state whether the plant can be put outside in the summer.
Humidity: information on the kind of air surrounding the plant.
Watering: the amount of water needed.
Fertilizing: intervals for treating with liquid fertilizer.
Pests: the most common pests are discussed.
Replanting: a particular time of

year is given for plants that have a dormant period.
Soil mixture: the ratios for mixing soil are given. The correct materials are fibrous, sieved peat, fine bark humus, loam baked to fine grains (obtainable from specialist bonsai nurseries) and lava sand containing grains up to 5 mm in diameter (from aquarium suppliers). Pumice sand can be used instead of lava sand. The soil mixtures given here have been tried out extensively and found to be the most suitable for bonsai (simple mixtures, see p. 23).
Pruning: the type of cut and the time.
Wiring: indicates the elasticity of the wood and whether it is suitable for wiring.
NB: this refers to special features of the plant.
Warning: refers to toxicity of plants or risk of injury.
My tip: special advice and tips on care.

Warning symbol
✝ This plant is toxic!

Araucaria excelsa (indoor fir)
This plant is not easy to shape. Only the topmost branches are willing to fork after cutting.

Mediterranean trees and shrubs

Mediterranean plants do not only originate from the countries that border the Mediterranean Sea. A typical Mediterranean climate is also to be found in south-western Australia, South Africa, Chile and California – places with dry summers and moist, relatively cool winters. Plants from these climatic zones are not very sensitive to the cold. As soon as there is no longer a risk of frost, you can place them outside in a semi-shady position that is sheltered from the wind. An awning draped over a railing will protect your plant from intense midday sunlight or strong winds.

Many woody Mediterranean plants have leaves with a waxy surface. This prevents them from losing too much water through evaporation. They can even cope with dry air in heated rooms.

Plants with delicate foliage will need cool overwintering. Plants such as pomegranates will lose their foliage in winter and will need to observe a dormancy phase even indoors, at temperatures between 4-10° C (39-50° F).

Conifers and *Cistus* species prefer a humid climate. Overwinter them at temperatures between 4-15° C (39-59° F) or make sure that you provide higher humidity for them when your rooms are heated (see p. 16).

A nineteen-year-old pomegranate tree that has been shaped as a bonsai for three years.

A visual delight – red Punica flowers.

These woody Mediterranean plants flower profusely.

Punica granatum "Nana"
Dwarf pomegranate

Origin: Asia Minor.
Care: relatively simple.
Position: during the summer, on an east- or west-acing windowsill, preferably outside. During the winter, -10° C (39-50° F) (the tree will lose its leaves). Thereafter, in a bright position at about 18° C (64° F) for two weeks, then at room temperature.
Humidity: high.
Watering: keep the soil medium moist, water sparingly during the winter dormancy period.
Fertilizing: from early spring to late summer every two weeks; from early to late autumn every four weeks.
Pests: susceptible to aphids and white fly.
Replanting: annually after the winter dormancy phase.
Soil mixture: 1 part peat, 3 parts humus, 2 parts loam, 1 part lava sand.
Pruning: cut back rigorously in the autumn. Do not prune during the summer as the flowers will appear on this year's wood.
Wiring: possible as the wood is pliable.
NB: the fruits are edible.

My tip: Pomegranates flower most profusely in direct sunlight. They should be planted in relatively large bowls or containers. This will prevent the soil from drying out too quickly.

1. *Cistus ladanifer*
2. *Cistus albidus*
3. *Cistus monspeliensis*

Origin: Mediterranean areas.
Care: difficult to overwinter.
Position: during the summer, as for pomegranates. During the winter, bright at 4-10° C (39-50° F). If only a dark cellar offers the right temperature, illuminate the plant with a bright plant lamp for nine hours a day.
Humidity: high.
Watering: plentifully.
Fertilizing: from mid-spring to late summer, once a week; from early autumn to early winter, every three weeks.
Pests: not very susceptible.
Replanting: annually, first month of spring.
Soil mixture: 3 parts humus, 2 parts loam, 1 part lava sand.
Pruning: cut back in the autumn. Do not cut in the summer if possible.
Wiring: possible as the wood is pliable.
Warning: *C. ladanifer* and *monospeliensis* have glandular hairs which could cause an allergic reaction.

My tip: Bonsai created from these three species should be at least 60 cm (24 in) tall so that they will produce masses of flowers.

These sclerophyllous evergreens are very easy to care for. They can also cope with dry, centrally heated air.

1. *Citrus limon*
   Lemon
2. *Pistacia lentiscus*
   Pistachio
3. *Quercus coccifera*
   Holly oak
4. *Rosmarinus officinalis*
   Rosemary
5. *Myrtus communis*
   Myrtle

Origin: Mediterranean areas.
Care: simple.
Position: during the summer, on an east- or west-facing windowsill outside. During the winter, in a south-facing window.
Humidity: normal.
Watering: keep soil slightly moist.
Fertilizing: early spring to late summer, every two weeks; from early autumn to late winter, every six weeks.
Pests: not very susceptible, except for *Citrus* species (scale insects).
Replanting: annually, preferably in the first month of spring.
Soil mixture: 3 parts humus, 2 parts loam, 1 part lava sand.
Pruning: cut back rigorously in the autumn. Do not cut too much off a lemon tree as there will then be no flowers. A pistachio tree can be cut back several times during the summer.
Cut holly oak a second time when the new young shoots start becoming woody during the last month of spring. This will result in denser branches. Cut back rosemary again after it has flowered. Myrtle flowers appear on this year's wood, so do not prune between early spring and mid-summer.
Wiring: possible as the wood of these species is pliable, except for rosemary which becomes brittle with advancing age; young shoots can, however, be wired quite easily.
NB: the tough, leathery leaves of these sclerophyllous evergreen plants will withstand extreme drought during the summer and can cope with very dry air in centrally heated rooms during the winter.

My tip: In the case of the lemon tree, only larger bonsai (over 50 cm/20 in) will flower profusely. The roots are sensitive to waterlogging. Make sure there is adequate drainage in tall containers. Lemon trees bought from a nursery should come in a pot and be equipped with a firm rootstock. They should cope quite happily with long-distance travel. The holly oak can be obtained at a specialist tree nursery. The best time to buy one is in early spring.

Conifers should be watered regularly.

The branches of the cypress exude a pleasant scent of lemons.

Pinus pinea
Umbrella pine

Origin: Mediterranean areas, Canary Islands.
Care: difficult; requires high humidity.
Position: during the summer, in an east- or west-facing window, preferably outside (semi-shade). During the winter, in a bright window. Ideal winter temperature: 10-15° C (50-59° F); provide plenty of humidity at higher temperatures.
Humidity: fairly high during the winter.
Watering: all year round, normal moisture.
Fertilizing: from early spring to early summer, every three to four weeks;

from mid-summer to late winter, every six to eight weeks.
Pests: not very susceptible; perhaps mealy bugs.
Replanting: every one to two years in late winter to mid-spring.
Soil mixture: 1 part peat, 3 parts humus, 2 parts loam, 2 parts lava sand.
Pruning: during early summer, cut back new shoots to 1-2 cm (¾ in); possibly repeating in the autumn.
Wiring: recommended. The wood is very pliable.
NB: resin will ooze from fresh cuts.

My tip: Water regularly. If the needles start to discolour, you may not be able to save the tree.

Cupressus macrocarpa
Californian cypress

Origin: coastal mountains of southern California.
Care: not very easy.
Position: during the summer, in an east- or west-facing window (semi-shade). During the winter, in a south-facing window.
Humidity: high.
Watering: all year round, very regularly, but keep the soil only just moist as the roots are sensitive to waterlogging.
Fertilizing: from early spring to early autumn every two to three weeks; from mid-autumn to late winter, every four to six weeks.
Pests: not very likely.

Replanting; every one to two years, preferably during the winter.
Soil mixture: 2 parts peat, 3 parts humus, 2 parts loam, 2 parts lava sand.
Pruning: only cut off entire branches; pick off the fine shoots. Prune during the summer, every six to eight weeks; during the winter, about every twelve weeks.
Wiring: possible. Young branches (diameter up to 3 mm) are very pliable. Thicker branches will need to be bent very gently as they snap easily.

My tip: During the winter, spray your cypress daily (in the morning) or stand the plant in a bonsai terrarium (see p. 16).

Woody plants from subtropical regions

Southern China, Taiwan and the southern islands of the Japanese archipelago experience a subtropical climate with humid, hot summers and mild winters with plenty of rain. The majority of imported indoor bonsai originate from these areas of the world, for example, *Carmona, Malphigia, Murraya, Podocarpus, Sageretia, Serissa* and the Japanese elm (*Ulmus parvifolia*). Bearing in mind the climatic conditions of their places of origin, these plants will require very high humidity. This means that during the winter they will need temperatures of around 15° C (59° F) or additional humidity will have to be provided. *Fuchsia, Cuphea* and *Jacobinia* originate from Central America. As a rule, they require the same care as the subtropical, woody plants of South East Asia. Some very robust indoor woody plants, such as *Corokia, Eucalyptus* and *Melaleuca*, originate from the subtropical regions of Australia and New Zealand.

Sageretia thea
twin-trunk bonsai
(SOKAN) in the slanting
style (SHAKAN). For
instructions on care, see
page 48.

Fuchsia magellanica
Fuchsia minutiflora
Fuchsia

Origin: more than 100 different species grow in Central and South America, New Zealand and Tahiti; countless hybrids and cultivars.
Care: relatively simple.
Position: in an east- or west-facing window, also outside during the summer (semi-shade). Overwintering in as cool a place as possible. Most species of *Fuchsia* lose their leaves during the winter and can be overwintered like dwarf pomegranates (see p. 41). More sensitive species of fuchsia, like *Fuchsia minutiflora*, should be placed in a bright position and provided with sufficient humidity for overwintering.
Humidity: medium.
Watering: normal. The rootstock should not be allowed to dry out.
Fertilizing: during mid-spring to early autumn, every three to four weeks.
Pests: white fly.
Replanting: annually after the winter dormancy phase (early to late spring).
Soil mixture: 2 parts peat, 1 part humus, 1 part loam, 1 part lava sand.
Pruning: rigorous cutting back in the autumn.
Wiring: possible as the wood is pliable.

My tip: Fuchsias do not like lime, so use soil containing peat and treat the water with a softening agent.

Fuchsia magellanica is hardy to -10° C (14° F).

Fuchsia minutiflora flowers nearly all year round.

The rather demanding Carmona.

The Serissa is covered in flowers in early summer.

Carmona microphylla

Origin: South East Asia.
Care: difficult.
Position: in summer, in an east- or west-facing window; from early summer to early autumn outside. During the winter, in a south-facing window at 10-18° C (50-64° F); if the temperature is higher, provide extra humidity.
Humidity: high.
Watering: very carefully and regularly. The roots are sensitive to both waterlogging and dryness.
Fertilizing: from late spring to early autumn, every two to three weeks; from mid-autumn to early spring, every four to six.
Pests: medium suscepti-bility to red spider mites, mildew and grey mould.
Replanting: every two to three years, in spring.
Soil mixture: 1 part peat, 2 parts humus, 2 parts loam, 1 part lava sand.
Pruning: twice annually, prune new growth back to two to three leaves.
Wiring: easy.
NB: the red fruits are not edible.

My tip: *Carmona* is often sold planted in pure clay. This kind of soil cannot be watered properly and should be exchanged for a better soil. Only the outer soil around the root sys-tem should be removed, however, as the roots are rather sensitive.

Serissa foetida
"Tree of a thousand stars"

Origin: South East Asia.
Care: not easy.
Position: in a very bright place, but not in direct, intense midday sun in summer; from early sum-mer to early autumn, out-side. During the winter, preferably at a tempera-ture of 10-15° C (50-59° F).
Humidity: very high.
Watering: abundantly, but avoid waterlogging. The roots are sensitive.
Fertilizing: from early spring to mid-autumn, every two weeks; from late autumn to late winter, every three to four weeks.
Pests: not very suscepti-ble, sometimes red spider mites.
Replanting: every one to two years.
Soil mixture: 1 part peat, 2 parts humus, 2 parts loam, 1 part lava sand.
Pruning: only shorten branches that have grown too long. This encourages the formation of lots of flowers.
Wiring: easy as the wood is very pliable.
NB: *Serissa* is covered with white, star-like flowe in early summer.

My tip: Unfortunately, thi plant is usually embedde in clay when you buy it. This must be exchanged for good soil (see p. 59).

The fruit of the dwarf orange tree is edible but sour.

A robust sclerophyllous evergreen.

Fortunella hindsii
Dwarf orange tree, Kumquat

Origin: Taiwan.
Care: relatively simple.
Position: bright, but not in intense midday sunlight. Also outside from early summer to mid-autumn.
Humidity: medium.
Watering: medium moist soil. Avoid waterlogging.
Fertilizing: from early spring to mid-autumn, every two weeks; from late autumn to late winter, every four to six weeks.
Pests: scale insects and mealy bugs.
Replanting: every two to three years, between early and mid-spring.
Soil mixture: 1 part peat, 2 parts humus, 2 parts loam, 1 part lava sand.
Pruning: only shorten branches that have grown too long, otherwise flowers and fruit will be lost.
Wiring: not very easy, as older wood is brittle.

My tip: Dwarf orange trees produce flowers and fruit on their one-year-old branches. A rigorous pruning will cause a loss of flowers and fruit for at least a year. Allow your bonsai to grow large (at least 50 cm/20 in) and give it a relatively large container. Only shorten the branches that have grown too long at the top and cut back the rest of the crown with restraint.

Pittosporum tobira

Origin: southern China, southern Japan, southern Korea.
Care: as for dwarf orange trees. The difference between these two species is more a matter of the style of shaping. *Pittosporum* is grown as a hedge in its countries of origin and in Mediterranean regions. In the rest of the world it is used as a large container plant. It can cope with any kind of pruning and, if the air is humid enough, it will produce shoots even if you have cut it back so much in the spring that no leaves were left. The flowers appear from late spring to early summer in the leaf axils produced the year before. If you wish your plant to flower, around the end of the first month of summer you should cut it back to one to five leaves on shoots that have grown since the last flowering, and then cut it no more.

My tip: Preferably allow your *Pittosporum* to grow to the size of a large garden bonsai (over 80 cm/32 in from the top of the bowl). These large plants will produce lots of flowers and will still look attractive even if the new shoots have grown rather long.

These species of woody plants can cope with dry, centrally heated air. They love a position outside during the summer.

1. *Grevillea robusta*
Australian silver oak
Origin: New South Wales, – Queensland (Australia).

2. *Sageretia thea*
False tea plant
Origin: southern China.

3. *Murraya paniculata*
Orange jasmine
Origin: South East Asia.

4. *Malphigia coccigera*
Barbados cherry
Origin: Caribbean islands.

5. *Ulmus parvifolia*
Japanese elm
Origin: China, Korea, Taiwan, Japan.

Care: simple.
Position: bright but no intense, direct midday sunlight during the summer. From early summer to early autumn, place outside in a semi-shady position sheltered from the wind. Can be overwintered at normal or even cool room temperatures (not below 12° C/54° F).
Humidity: normal.
Fertilizing: from early spring to early autumn, every two to three weeks; from mid-autumn to late winter, every four to six.
Pests: the species with delicate leaves, like *Grevillea*, Sageretia and *Ulmus*, are susceptible to white fly. Infestation with red spider mites is possi-

ble in all species.
Replanting: every one to two years, in spring.
Soil mixture: 1 part peat, 3 parts humus, 2 parts loam, 1 part lava sand.
Pruning: *Grevillea* and *Murraya* grow slowly and have large leaves. Prune only twice annually; large leaves can be trimmed. *Malphigia* flowers on one-year-old twigs (from early to late summer). Do not prune between early spring and late summer or flowers will be lost. *Sageretia* and *Ulmus* grow very fast. Cut back new growth three to six times a year to two to five pairs of leaves (*Sageretia*) or single leaves (*Ulmus*).
Wiring: apart from

Malphigia, all the species mentioned are easy to wire.
NB: Murraya flowers from late spring to early summer

My tip: Grevillea does not willingly form many branches as a young plant. The best specimens of this species are large container plants at least 1 m (40 in) tall. *Sageretia* and *Ulmus* are quite robust and will survive even serious mistakes in care: if they have lost leaves through lack of water, they can usually be saved by pulling a large plastic bag over them and watering abundantly. The "hood" should not be removed until new buds appear.

This Japanese azalea has enchanting pink flowers.

The roots of the South Sea myrtle must not dry out.

Rhododendron ✝
japonicum
Japanese azalea

Origin: southern and central Japan.
Care: relatively simple.
Position: bright, but not intense, direct sunlight. During the summer, place in the garden in a semishady position.
Humidity: normal.
Watering: abundantly. The roots must never dry out.
Fertilizing: all year round, every two to three weeks.
Pests: not very likely.
Replanting: annually, right after flowering.
Soil mixture: 3 parts peat, 1 part humus, 1 part loam, 1 part lava sand.
Pruning: only once a year

(from late spring to early summer), after which the new flowerbuds will start to form. Shorten the new shoots to one to three leaves; it is possible to cut back into old wood.
Wiring: not quite so easy.
NB: depending on the variety, it flowers from midautumn to early spring.
Warning: Rhododendrons may contain toxins.
My tip: The Japanese azalea is an ideal subject for your own first attempts at shaping a bonsai. It will flourish if you plant it in a peaty flowerbed in a semishady, moist place during the summer. It can easily be planted in a bowl in the autumn.

Leptospermum scoparium
South Sea myrtle

Origin: Australia.
Care: relatively simple.
Position: during the summer, in an east- or westfacing window; during the winter, in a south-facing window.
Humidity: medium.
Watering: very carefully. The sensitive roots must never be allowed to dry out.
Fertilizing: from late winter to early autumn, every two weeks; from midautumn to mid-winter, every four weeks.
Pests: not susceptible.
Replanting: annually after flowering (from late spring

to early summer).
Soil mixture: 2 parts peat, 2 parts humus, 1 part loam, 1 part lava sand.
Pruning: rigorous cutting back after flowering, but do not prune after midautumn, to allow flowerbuds to form.
Wiring: very easy.

My tip: If you plant *Leptospermum* in a relatively tall container, the risk of drying out is minimized. The small, tough leaves will not show any signs of lack of water until it is almost too late. Check whether the leaves are slightly curled at the edges – a symptom of an acute lack of water.

Syzygium prefers a semi-shady position.

Sophora likes a bright, but not too dry, position.

Syzygium paniculatum
Cherry myrtle

Origin: Australia.
Care: relatively simple.
Position: bright. Also outside from early summer to early autumn.
Humidity: medium. If it is to be overwintered at room temperatures, spray daily (mornings) from mid-autumn to mid-spring.
Watering: abundantly, but avoid waterlogging.
Fertilizing: from early spring to early autumn, every two weeks; from mid-autumn to late winter, every four to six weeks.
Pests: not very susceptible.
Replanting: every one to two years.
Soil mixture: 1 part peat, 3 parts humus, 2 parts loam, 1 part lava sand.
Pruning: a thorough pruning is possible soon after flowering is over, but do not prune again after early autumn.
Wiring: easy.
NB: flowers from mid-spring to early summer. The fruits are edible.

My tip: The plant should not be smaller than 60 cm (24 in) tall and should possess a well-developed crown. Young plants should be grown in a large container for several years, until they are about 1.5 m (60 in) tall, after which you can begin to shape them into bonsai.

Sophora tetraptera

Origin: New Zealand.
Care: relatively simple. The plant is easy to shape.
Position: very bright. During the summer, preferably outside in full sunlight. During the winter, in a cool, frost-free place, such as an unheated hallway or greenhouse.
Humidity: medium.
Watering: keep normally moist. If it is overwintered in a cool position, the tree will lose its foliage and will require only sparing amounts of water.
Fertilizing: from early spring to early autumn, every two weeks; from mid-autumn to late winter, every four to six weeks.
Pests: not very susceptible
Replanting: annually.
Soil mixture: 1 part peat, 3 parts humus, 2 parts loam, 1 part lava sand.
Pruning: a thorough pruning after flowering is over. You can cut back into old wood.
Wiring: easy as the wood is very pliable.
NB: will flower in late winter if overwintered in a cool position.

My tip: Sophora requires lots of sunlight. You should use a very large, tall bonsai container if the bonsai is placed in intense direct sunlight during the summer. This will prevent the soil from drying out too quickly.

Corokias are resistant to drought.

Podocarpus cannot cope with lime.

Corokia buddleioides
Corokia (four species)

Origin: New Zealand.
Care: simple.
Position: bright to full sunlight.
Humidity: no special requirements.
Watering: keep the soil medium moist.
Fertilizing: from early spring to early autumn, every three weeks; from mid-autumn to late winter, every four to six weeks.
Pests: not very susceptible.
Replanting: every one to two years.
Soil mixture: 3 parts humus, 2 parts loam, 2 parts lava sand.
Pruning: several times a year, cut back new growth to two to five leaves.
Wiring: easy as the wood is pliable.
NB: *Corokia* can be overwintered in a cool, frost-free place or in normal room temperatures. It will even survive dried-out soil.

My tip: It is mainly the species *Corokia cotoneaster* that you will find for sale in the bonsai trade but you will find all four species of *Corokia* in flower shops that sell large container plants. They are ideal subjects for your first attempts at bonsai shaping because of their pliable wood, favourable response to cutting back and easy requirements for care.

Podocarpus macrophyllus
Stone yew

Origin: southern Japan.
Care: relatively simple.
Position: in an east- or west-facing window; from early summer to early autumn, also outside in semi-shade.
Humidity: medium. Spray the plant every morning if it is overwintered at room temperature.
Watering: medium. Never let it dry out.
Fetilizing: from early spring to early autumn, every two to three weeks; from mid-autumn to late winter, every four to six.
Pests: not very susceptible.
Replanting: every two to three years.
Soil mixture: 3 parts humus, 2 parts loam, 1 part lava sand.
Pruning: shorten new growth to a few centimetres.
Wiring: possible, as the young branches are quite pliable. Be careful when bending older wood.
NB: The genus *Podocarpus* only occurs in the southern hemisphere. It contains about 100 species. One often finds various *Podocarpus* species in tree nurseries in Mediterranean areas. They are all easy to care for.

My tip: Use very hard water for watering this species.

Woody plants from tropical regions

The tropical rain forests are home to a huge number of tree species which will flourish in centrally heated rooms. The reason for this is the special climatic conditions of their natural habitats: in the mornings, the sun shines fiercely and the plants' leaves would dry out if they were not covered with a waxy layer. In the afternoons, tropical thunderstorms cool everything down again with torrents of rain.

Rain-forest trees may grow very old and very tall. Young plants have to survive on the sparse amount of light that manages to penetrate to the forest floor, which is why tropical plants kept indoors can manage on little light. They can even cope occasionally with soil that is too moist, as long as it is loose enough for air to penetrate it.

The only real problem with care is if the water is too hard. The soil on the rain-forest floor is very rich in humus and practically lime-free, so all of these plants will react to high chalk or lime levels with symptoms of chlorosis.

▲ *Ficus retusa that is 60 cm (24 in) tall:*
This tree probably grew to a height of 6 m (10 ft) before it was shaped into bonsai.

1. *Ficus retusa crassifolia*
2. *Ficus r. nitida*
3. *Ficus neriifolia*
4. *Ficus inversa*
5. *Ficus benjamina*
6. *Ficus buxifolia*
7. *Ficus benjamina "Starlight"*

Origin: the tropical zones of the world.
Care: simple.
Position: east- or west-facing window, no intense sunlight.
Humidity: normal.
Watering: abundantly, with lime-free water.
Fertilizing: from early spring to early autumn, every two to three weeks; from mid-autumn to late winter, every four to six weeks.
Pests: not very susceptible with good care. Weakened plants are prone to attack by aphids, mealy bugs, scale insects and red spider mites.
Replanting: every one to two years.
Soil mixture: 3 parts peat, 1 part humus, 1 part loam, 1½ parts lava sand.
Pruning: cut back branches that have grown too long to one to two leaves.
Wiring: easy. Remove the wire after six months.
NB: apply a drop of water to cut surfaces. This helps the milky sap to curdle and harden.

My tip: When cutting young branches, leave a short section of branch above the last leaf, so that there is no risk of the branch drying out.

The tropical Ficus species make ideal indoor plants.

Ficus pumila likes to have "wet feet".

This species of Ficus can manage with little light.

Ficus pumila
Climbing fig

Origin: North Vietnam, southern China, southern Japan, Riukiu Islands, Taiwan.
Care: very simple.
Position: bright, but not intense, sunlight.
Humidity: medium.
Watering: abundantly.
Fertilizing: from early spring to early autumn, every two to three weeks; from mid-autumn to late winter, every four to six weeks.
Pests: not very susceptible.
Replanting: every two to three weeks.
Soil mixture: 3 parts peat, 1 part humus, 1 part loam, 1½ parts lava sand.

Pruning: cut back long branches to one to three leaves.
Wiring: easy, the climbing fig is a flexible, creeper-like plant.
NB: climbing fig will even grow in water.

My tip: Climbing figs are generally shaped in the cascade style. Shaping them to look like indigenous ivy creates a particularly attractive effect: use wire to fix a piece of bog root (which will not rot and is obtainable from aquarium suppliers) in the bonsai bowl and tie the climbing fig to it with raffia. Wire the lateral branches to protrude horizontally and prune regularly.

Ficus schlechteri

Origin: southern Asia.
Care: simple. Needs little light.
Position: north-, east- or west-facing windows; no direct sunlight.
Humidity: medium.
Watering: keep the soil constantly moist.
Fertilizing: from early spring to early autumn, every two to three weeks; from mid-autumn to late winter, every four to six.
Pests: sometimes attracts red spider mites.
Replanting: every one to two years.
Soil mixture: 3 parts peat, 1 part humus, 1 part loam, 1½ parts lava sand.
Pruning: cut back young

branches that have grown too long to one to three leaves.
Wiring: easy (pliable wood). Remove the wire after six months as the shoots are quite delicate.
NB: this species of fig tree grows in the undergrowth of rain forests. It will grow indoors without extra light.
My tip: *Ficus schlechteri* i easy to train to grow over a porous lava stone. To de this, remove the soil from the tops of the roots, train the roots across the stone tie them in position with raffia and place the arrangement in a transparent plastic bag containing a little soil until the plant has rooted again properly

A robust and very beautiful Schefflera.

The ming aralia is a plant for the experts.

Schefflera actinophylla

Origin: north-eastern Australia, New Guinea.
Care: simple.
Position: very bright, but no intense direct sunlight in summer.
Humidity: medium.
Watering: medium. Do not allow the rootstock to dry out.
Fertilizing: medium. From mid-spring to early autumn, every four weeks; from mid-autumn to early spring, every six to eight weeks.
Pests: not very susceptible.
Replanting: every two years.
Soil mixture: 2 parts peat, 2 parts humus, 1 part loam, 1½ parts lava sand.

Pruning: all the shoots will grow vertically, so they can be shortened to the desired height at any time. *Schefflera* will also shoot willingly from bare wood.
Wiring: difficult as the wood is not pliable.
NB: *Schefflera* are often sold growing on a lava stone.
I recommend standing these plants on a tray filled with gravel or Hortag (see p. 17).

My tip: *Schefflera* can be cut back to bare wood and then covered with a transparent plastic bag until new leaves have formed.

Polyscias fruticosa
Ming aralia

Origin: tropical regions of Asia.
Care: rather complicated.
Position: as bright as possible, but no direct midday sunlight.
Humidity: very high.
Watering: abundantly. Avoid waterlogging.
Fertilizing: from early spring to early autumn, every two to three weeks; from mid-autumn to late winter, every four to six weeks.
Pests: not very susceptible.
Replanting: every two years.
Soil mixture: 1 part peat, 3 parts humus, 2 parts loam, 2 parts lava sand.

Pruning: cut back shoots that have grown too long to one to three pairs of leaves.
Wiring: possible as the wood is pliable.
NB: at least six species of *Polyscias* are for sale in flower shops and garden centres. They all have the same requirements for care.

My tip: You can cultivate this plant successfully in a bonsai terrarium (see p. 16). Before planting, insert a finger-width drainage layer of fine Hortag or lime-free aquarium gravel on the bottom of the bowl, so that water can drain away easily from the plant container.

Plants that originate from dry steppes and desert plains

The plant species introduced here are recommended for newcomers to indoor bonsai as they create hardly any problems with respect to care. Tropical, dry plains or steppes have only one or two short rainy seasons per year. Plants with organs for storing water, or possessing long tap roots that reach down to the ground water table, are able to survive these long periods of drought. They require a very bright window position and soil containing plenty of oxygen. Some of these species can even cope with drying out completely for several days, until the water-storing leaves begin to look wrinkled or delicate leaves begin to fall. If you water carefully after such an event and then gradually increase the amount of water given (over a period of two to three weeks), these plants will react with the spontaneous formation of branching shoots and a profusion of flowers. The time of greatest growth for most of these succulents is the dry months from mid- to late summer; they usually flower from late in the winter to early spring.

Portulacaria afra

A bush-type Portulacaria from South Africa in the informal upright style (MOYOGI). (Instructions for care, see p. 58.)

Sarcocaulon rigidum
Bushman's candle

Origin: Namibia.
Care: simple.
Position: sunny.
Humidity: low.
Watering: medium.
Fertilizing: every four to six weeks.
Pests: grey mould.
Replanting: every two years.
Soil mixture: 3 parts humus, 2 parts loam, 2 parts lava sand.
Pruning: rigorous cutting back is possible.
Wiring: possible.
NB: this plant flowers all year round but the flowers will only open in sunlight.
Warning: there is a risk of injury from the long thorns on the plant.

My tip: Cut the thorns off before you start shaping.

Adenium obesum ✝
Desert rose

Origin: East Africa.
Care: simple.
Position: sunny.
Humidity: low.
Watering: medium.
Fertilizing: every four weeks.
Pests: grey mould.
Replanting: every two years.
Soil mixture: 3 parts humus, 2 parts loam, 2 parts lava sand.
Pruning: cut back rigorously after flowering is over.
Wiring: possible.
Warning: the sap of the desert rose is highly toxic.

Beautiful flowers all year round.

Adenium obesum produces a profusion of flowers.

The only requirements of woody plants from tropical dry plains are a bright position and restrained watering.

1. Crassula arborescens
Origin: South Africa.

2. Euphorbia balsamifera
Origin: Canary Islands, west Africa.

3. Euphorbia milii
Origin: Madagascar.

4. Trichodiadema stellatum
Origin: South Africa.

5. Brachychiton rupestris
Bottle tree
Origin: Australia.

Care: simple.
Position: sunny, outside in summer but not if there is much heavy rain.
Humidity: low.
Watering: keep the soil reasonably moist.
Fertilizing: every four weeks.
Pests: almost never susceptible to infestation by animal pests. If humidity becomes too high, there is a risk of grey mould.
Replanting: every two years.
Soil mixture: 3 parts humus, 2 parts loam, 2 parts lava sand.
Pruning: cutting back into old wood is possible in all species.
Wiring: possible. Wire the plant parts without exerting too much pressure.

Warning: all *Euphorbia* species contain a milky sap that is extremely irritating to the skin and mucous membranes.

My tip: If you keep it dry for four to six weeks during high summer, *Crassula* will flower from late winter to early spring.
Euphorbia balsamifera will spontaneously form forked branches if it dries out briefly (for a week) in high summer. New branches that are too long should be cut back. The sap that oozes from the plant will not harm it.
Euphorbia milii is easy to shape and wire as long as

you cut off all the thorns beforehand and spray the plant with water to dispel the milky sap. Begin to shape the plant next day. *Trichodiadema* forms thick tap roots instead of a stem. Plant this small tree in such a way that the main part of the tuber is visible. The soft branches are easy to wire.
Brachychiton will only form branches if you cut back right into the old wood. You should allow two to three leaves to remain on the stumps of branches, so that the plant cannot dry out. The gnarled, water-storing neck of the root should be free of soil and clearly visible.

The exotic Rhapis excelsa.

A little group of palms makes a beautiful feature.

Rhapis excelsa
Rhapis humilis

Origin: south-eastern China; imported into Taiwan and southern Japan.

Care: not quite so simple; cool overwintering will be necessary.

Position: very bright but no direct midday sun from early summer to the first month of autumn. From late autumn to late winter, the temperature should not rise above 12-15° C (54-59° F). It will be sufficient to overwinter the plant in cool, frost-free conditions.

Humidity: fairly high but it not a good idea to place the plant in a bonsai terrarium. *Rhapis* species like fresh air. They may also become infested with pests.

Watering: abundantly, but avoid waterlogging. The roots are sensitive.

Fertilizing: from early spring to early autumn, every two weeks; from mid-autumn to late winter, every four to six weeks.

Pests: susceptible to infestation with mealy bugs.

Replanting: annually, preferably in late winter to mid-spring.

Soil mixture: 1 part peat, 3 parts humus, 2 parts loam, 1 part lava sand.

Pruning: completely remove fronds that have grown too long. Palms will not form branches.

Wiring: possible, but not recommended.

NB: *Rhapis* palms react to air that is too dry and warm (for example, centrally heated air) by producing brown leaf tips. Fungal infections may invade these parts. Remove discoloured fronds immediately and stand the palm in a cooler position.

My tip: This genus can form stolons. The only suitable style for this plant is the group style (YOSE-UE).

These two *Rhapis* species are often offered for sale planted in almost pure clay. Make sure to exchange this very unsuitable soil for the correct kind of bonsai soil for this genus. First remove the outer surface of the clay (about two to three fingers' width) and replace it with bonsai soil. About six months later, you can remove further lumps of clay from the inner portions of the rootstock. Work very carefully when doing this so that you inflict as little damage as possible on the fibrous root system. If you remove some of the fronds at the same time, you will be able to trim the root much more easily.

Index

Figures in bold indicate illustrations.

Index

Addresses

Useful addresses in the UK

Federation of British Bonsai Societies
52 Ashburn Road, Heaton, Norris, Stockport, Cheshire SK4 2PU

British Bonsai Association
23 Nimrod Road, Streatham, London SW16 6SZ

Scottish Bonsai Association
22 Buccleugh Street, Edinburgh EH8 9IL

Useful international addresses

Australia

National Bonsai Association
22 Burraga Avenue, Terrey Hills, New South Wales 2084

European Bonsai Association
G.M. De Beule, Groenstraat 28, B-9170, Waasmunster, Belgium

Germany

Paul Lesniewicz, Manneheim Straat 401, 6900 Heidelburg

South Africa

Shibui Bonsai Kai, PO Box 81084, Parkhurst 2120

Useful addresses in the USA

Bonsai Institute of California, PO Box 78211, Los Angeles, CA 90016-1211

W.M. Valavanis, 412 Pinnacle Road, Rochester, NY 14623

UK sources of specialist material

Hewett and Stewart, 91 Epsom Road, Morden, Surrey (mail order)

Hilliers and Sons, Winchester, Hampshire SO22 5DN

Mount Pleasant Trees, Rockhampton, Berkeley, Gloucestershire

Author's note

This guide is concerned with the care and shaping of indoor bonsai. Some of the plants described here have spines and thorns which can cause injuries. The plant descriptions (pp. 9-59) point out any risk of injury. Plants which may cause injuries should be kept in positions that are inaccessible to children or pets. The milky sap of *Ficus* and *Euphorbia* species can cause allergies in some people. Information about this is given in the relevant sections (pp. 39-59). People who suffer from contact allergies should definitely wear gloves when they are handling these plants.

Some of the plants described here bear fruits, some of which are edible. This information is also given in the plant descriptions. Please endeavour to make absolutely certain that children and pets do not eat any of the non-edible fruits as they may cause considerable health problems.

Ulmus parvifolia (Japanese elm) shaped in the slanting style (SHAKAN).

Cover photographs

Front cover main picture: *Acer palmatum, in autumn colours, in a blue ceramic pot*; top right: *70-year-old Crataegus coccinea*; middle right: *Berried Cotoneaster horizontalis*; bottom right: *200-year-old Chamaecyparis obtusa.*
Inside front cover: *Red-flowering rhododendron and Ficus retusa.*
Inside back cover: *Japanese elm (Ulmus parvifolia) in the slanting style (SHAKAN).*
Back cover: *A mature and diverse bonsai collection.*

Photographic acknowledgements

Bajohr: 41/3; Dinter: 41/2; Garnweidner: 42/5; Jacqui Hurst, Garden Picture Library: front cover main picture; König: 42/2; Lamontagne, Garden Picture Library: back cover; Layer: 42/1; Mein Schöner Garten/Stork: 3, 18, 19, 22, 26, 31, 32, 34, 35/1-3; Pfisterer: 8, 28, 29, 48/4, 55 right; Photos Horticultural: front cover top and bottom right; Howard Rice, Garden Picture Library: front cover middle right; Riedmiller: 11 bottom, 13 left, 15, 44, 52, 59; Schmidt-Thomé: 38; Schulz: 41/1; Strauss: 58; Wothe: 42/3; Stork: all others.

This edition published 1999 by
Merehurst Limited
Ferry House, 51–57 Lacy Road,
Putney, London SW15 1PR

© 1989 Gräfe und Unzer GmbH, Munich

ISBN 1-85391-724-9

English text copyright ©
Merehurst Limited 1994
Translated by Astrid Mick
Edited by Lesley Young
Design/typesetting by Paul Cooper Design
Printed in Hong Kong by Wing King Tong